GUARDED GIRLS

ALSO BY CHARLOTTE CORBEIL-COLEMAN

The End of Pretending (with Emily Sugerman)
Twisted (with Joseph Jomo Pierre)

GUARDED GIRLS

CHARLOTTE CORBEIL-COLEMAN

PLAYWRIGHTS CANADA PRESS
TORONTO

For professional or amateur production rights, please contact:
Colin Rivers, Marquis Literary
312-73 Richmond St. W., Toronto, ON M5H 4E8
416.960.9123, info@mqlit.ca, www.mqlit.ca

LIBRARY AND ARCHIVES CANADA CATALOGUING IN PUBLICATION
Title: Guarded girls / Charlotte Corbeil-Coleman.
Names: Corbeil-Coleman, Charlotte, author.
Description: A play.
Identifiers: Canadiana (print) 20190153032
| Canadiana (ebook) 20190153059 | ISBN 9780369100436 (softcover)
| ISBN 9780369100443 (PDF) | ISBN 9780369100450 (EPUB)
| ISBN 9780369100467 (MOBI)
Classification: LCC PS8555.O595 G83 2019 | DDC C812/.6—dc23

Playwrights Canada Press acknowledges that we operate on land, which, for thousands of years, has been the traditional territories of the Mississaugas of the Credit, Huron-Wendat, Anishinaabe, Métis, and Haudenosaunee peoples. Today, this meeting place is home to many Indigenous peoples from across Turtle Island and we are grateful to have the opportunity to work and play here.

We acknowledge the financial support of the Canada Council for the Arts—which last year invested $153 million to bring the arts to Canadians throughout the country—the Ontario Arts Council (OAC), Ontario Creates, and the Government of Canada for our publishing activities.

Canada Council
for the Arts
Conseil des arts
du Canada

ONTARIO ARTS COUNCIL
CONSEIL DES ARTS DE L'ONTARIO
an Ontario government agency
un organisme du gouvernement de l'Ontario

ONTARIO | ONTARIO
CREATES | CRÉATIF

FOREWORD

by Senator Kim Pate

Guarded Girls provides incredibly moving and disturbingly accurate glimpses into the chilling and too often devastating impacts of imprisonment on girls and women, whether they are staff, prisoners, or the family members of the caged or warders. An important part of the play is situated in segregation, also known as solitary confinement or "the hole."

Charlotte Corbeil-Coleman links together a number of highly descriptive and diverse vignettes into a compelling compilation that propels her audience into a world that is rarely exposed to the public. Whether you read the play's script or watch actors bring Charlotte's words to life, you will not escape the reality of the irreparable damage done to individuals and relationships by the discrimination and dysfunction of the penal system, especially the permanent and brutal physiological, psychological, and social damage caused by the isolation of prisoners in segregation.

Guarded Girls mimics, in real time, some of what happened to Ashley Smith before she died nearly twelve years ago in a segregation cell in a federal penitentiary, Grand Valley prison for women. As the character Sid's angst, insecurity, and fear emerge as bravado and defensive aggression, we see how the guard often misunderstands and reacts to her. We can imagine how Ashley's typically adolescent rebellious language and behaviour were similarly reinterpreted by correctional staff and others as "bad" and "criminal." We can also recognize the escalation of consequences and resulting degradation of spirit and mental health.

The play hints at the systemic nature of the class, race, and gender biases that contribute to women being the fastest growing prison population, and to the fact that 40% of women in prison, and the majority of those who are segregated, are Indigenous and have significant mental health issues. The play clearly reveals the lack of supports for children and youth and how those too often form a direct link between child welfare involvement and criminalization.

Guarded Girls also illustrates the ways in which inadequate economic, social, and educational opportunities are compounded by a "correctional" system that belies its moniker. Scenes depict the ways in which staff are encouraged to overlook the humanity of those in their charge. These scenes are interspersed with those of a now paranoid staff who misconstrue prisoners' fears and concerns, and misjudge even compassion and mental deterioration. The play underscores the consequent mistrust between guards and those they guard. It thereby highlights genuine manifestations of systemic dysfunction bred by a system that, regardless of rhetoric to the contrary, too often privileges coercive control and punishment over more proactive interventions and rehabilitative approaches.

As Martin Morrow described the play in his review for *The Globe and Mail*, "The overall effect is like a time-lapse depiction of the torture of solitary confinement." I agree. Each time I watched the play, once with Ashley Smith's mother and sister, I experienced emotional and sometimes excruciating memories of the experiences of women, their children, and the staff who work in prisons.

Too often, the pains of imprisonment and the torture of isolation and separation are hidden by softer, kinder, and gentler words, intentions, and depictions. The banality of the ways that power and control can contort and corrupt are cloaked in individualized explanations of personal failings and wrongdoing. Members of the public, politicians, and playwrights alike may be forgiven for wishing that training and good intentions could change systems and cultures. Many B-grade movies, sensationalist texts, and inadequate pieces of legislation underscore this reality.

Most recently, the Senate of Canada amended a piece of federal legislation whose aim the government argued was to end the use of segregation in federal penitentiaries. Acknowledging the culture of rights denial within prisons, the Senate amended Bill C-83 to require that correctional authorities privilege the use of non-carceral approaches for Indigenous and other racialized prisoners, as well as those with disabling mental health and intellectual issues.

The Senate also sought to ensure that corrections reduce and eventually eliminate the use of isolation through a requirement that they apply to court for permission to segregate an individual for more than forty-eight hours. This judicial oversight would have allowed courts to ensure that the constitutional rights of prisoners were upheld. Former Supreme Court Justice Louise Arbour recommended such a measure in order to shift the existing rights-resistant correctional culture toward one of transparency, due process, and accountability. Unfortunately, these amendments were rejected by the government.

It has been nearly twelve years since Ashley Smith died in a segregation cell as the guards responsible for her care looked on, yet women and men continue to be incarcerated in the same conditions of isolation, known by Correctional Service Canada to cause irreparable psychological harm. When the government chose to reject the Senate amendments to Bill C-83, corrections was permitted to remain the only institution within the criminal legal system that is not accountable to the judiciary, and by extension, the public.

It is fitting that *Guarded Girls* is emerging during a time when Canada and many other countries are questioning the manner in which we criminalize and imprison the most economically, racially, socially, and personally marginalized. The Supreme Court of Canada is poised to rule on the use of isolation, solitary confinement, and other forms of segregation. I hope all who have the privilege, authority, and ability to impact these issues meet and listen to those who are inside and experiencing the realities so brilliantly and poignantly illustrated by Charlotte Corbeil-Coleman's *Guarded Girls*. It is a must read, as well as a must see!

The Honourable Kim Pate, C.M.
Senator

AUTHOR'S PREFACE

This play was created with research, interviews, and imagination. It's easy not to look at our prison system. Looking at it means engaging with a lot of hard questions about our society and ourselves. The people who spoke with me wanted the women's prison system to be seen. This play is a tiny piece of witnessing. There are a lot more stories from a lot more people that need to be told on this subject matter.

As this play was premiering, I was preparing for the birth of my first child. Because of this, I was thinking a lot about what we pass on to our children and what cycles, as parents, we must try to break. *Guarded Girls* is, in part, about how hard it is to try to break a cycle, whether it be in ourselves, our families, our institutions, or in our society.

This play is dedicated to everyone who is trying.

NOTES

In Canada, the legacy of genocide, stolen land, broken treaties, residential schools, relocation, systematic racism, and erasure is evident in the statistics regarding the women's prison system. According to a 2017 report by the Correctional Investigator of Canada, Indigenous women account for 38% of women incarcerated, while they make up less than 5% of the Canadian population.

Wherever possible, the cast should reflect or be in conversation with those who are represented in the prison system of the country or community that this play is being produced in. If it makes sense for you to change/omit culturally specific references (Kitchener, Ontario, Toronto) so that the play connects more with the audience, that is okay by me.

A pod is a prison cell.
A screw is a guard.
Seg is segregation/solitary confinement.
When Sid says "I want to tie up" she is referring to self-strangulation by putting a ligature around her neck.
Silences can be played as beats, pauses, or breaths.
A forward slash (/) indicates an overlap.
An em dash (—) indicates a cut-off.

Guarded Girls was originally commissioned by Green Light Arts and was developed in collaboration with the Tarragon Theatre. It was first produced by Tarragon Theatre in association with Green Light Arts in Toronto from March 26–May 5, 2019. It was then produced at the Registry Theatre, in Kitchener, Ontario, from May 8–19, 2019, with the same cast and creative team:

Guard: Columpa C. Bobb
Sid, CO1, Girl1: Vivien Endicott-Douglas
Brit, CO2, Girl3: Virgilia Griffith
Kit, Girl2: Michaela Washburn

Director: Richard Rose
Set and Costume Designer: Joanna Yu
Lighting Designer: André du Toit
Sound Designer: Thomas Ryder Payne
Stage Manager: Natasha Bean-Smith
Assistant Director: Audrey Dwyer
Assistant Designer (Set and Costume): Julia Kim
Intimacy and Fight Director: Siobhan Richardson

CHARACTERS

Sid, nineteen, inmate
Brit, twenty-three, inmate

Guard, mid-thirties to mid-forties, correctional officer

Kit, thirties, inmate at Grand Valley Institution for Women
CO1, correctional officer
CO2, correctional officer

Girl1, nine to thirteen years old
Girl2, thirteen to nineteen years old
Girl3, nine to thirteen years old

Sid, CO1, and Girl1 can be played by the same actor. Britt, CO2, and Girl3 can played by the same actor. Kit and Girl2 can be played by the same actor.

SET

The set is open to interpretation. I pictured a wall of buckets. If you picture something else, go with it. I encourage you to use your imagination as long as the prison is abstract—something felt as opposed to anything too literal. The leak in the ceiling is important, but where you go with it us up for interpretation as well. When the guard finds the objects, I encourage playfulness.

In a theatre, on a stage, there is a leak. The leak comes from the roof. Small drops of water fall to the stage.

It is not extreme but the sound of water hitting ground is noticeable and constant.

A woman dressed as a GUARD walks on stage with a bucket; she places it under the leak. She looks out to the audience.

ONE

Prison. BRIT sits alone, holding her knees to her chest.

SID walks in. She sits down, back to back, with BRIT. The light is tight around them. SID plays with a long, thin piece of fabric, what could be a torn bedsheet. She rubs it between her fingers for comfort. They both say nothing for quite some time. When they do speak it is rapid-fire fast.

BRIT: HEY.
SID: HEY.

Silence.

There's a leak.
BRIT: Yeah.

Silence.

I'm Britton.
SID: I know who you are.

Silence.

Everyone knows who you are.

Silence.

I'm Sid.
BRIT: Like Sidney?
SID: Like Sid.
BRIT: Cool.

Silence.

SID: I'm going to call you Brit.
BRIT: I prefer Britton.
SID: I bet, Brit.

BRIT: What do you like?
SID: Like?
BRIT: Like.

Silence.

SID: I like gum.
BRIT: Me too!
SID: I like putting so much gum in my mouth I can't talk—
BRIT: I could fit a whole pack of gum in my mouth—
SID: Me too. Me too.

Silence.

I guess I also like—giraffes.
BRIT: Why?
SID: Because their necks are so fucking long.
BRIT: That's an excellent reason. What do you hate?

Silence.

I hate glitter. I imagine it all over my body and it hurts.

SID: I hate tights.
BRIT: Like nylons?
SID: I hate pulling them up.
BRIT: So, would you like, like footless tights?
SID: No, 'cause you still got to pull them up and they're tight.

BRIT: I get that.

Silence.

Is this your first transfer?
SID: Nah, I been all over Canada.
BRIT: Yeah.
SID: Yeah.
BRIT: I've just been here.
SID: Yeah.

Silence.

What's it like?
BRIT: Here?
SID: Yeah.
BRIT: Bad. What's it like there?
SID: Out there?
BRIT: No, in here, but in the other places?

SID: Bad.

Silence.

BRIT: Where are you from?

Silence.

I'm from the Toon.

Beat.

Saskatoon.

Silence.

Are you from Toronto—
SID: Let's play a game.
BRIT: I don't like games.
SID: This is a good game.
BRIT: I don't play cards.
SID: It's not cards.
BRIT: I always lose at cards.
SID: It's not cards.
BRIT: I'm not a good loser.
SID: You can't lose at this.
BRIT: You can always lose.

    SID laughs.

SID: . . . You be me and I'll be you.
BRIT: . . . Okay.

    Beat.

How do I do it?
SID: Just . . . be me.
BRIT: *(thinks for a moment)* Okay.

    Beat.

SID: . . . Are you doing it?

    BRIT changes her face.

BRIT: Yeah.
SID: How does it feel?
BRIT: . . . It's . . . okay.
SID: Try harder.

BRIT stiffens her body.

BRIT: Okay. I'm being you. Yeah, I'm you.
SID: How does it feel?
BRIT: It's pretty intense.
SID: I know, RIGHT.

BRIT: What now?
SID: Start again.
BRIT: Again.
SID: Again. But. I'll be you.

Hey.
BRIT: HEY.

Beat.

SID: *(whispers)* There's a leak.
BRIT: *(nods understanding)* There's a leak.
SID: Yeah.

SID: I'm BRITTON.

BRIT laughs. SID waits.

BRIT: . . . I know who you are.

Beat.

I'm Sid.

SID: Like Sidney?

BRIT: Like Sid.

SID: Cool.

BRIT: I'm going to call you BRIT.

SID: *(in a snooty voice)* I prefer Britton.

BRIT: Hey, I didn't—

SID: What do you love?

BRIT: I said like.

SID: What do you like?

BRIT: Like?

SID: Like.

BRIT: I like gum.

SID: Me too!

BRIT: I like putting so much gum in my mouth I can't—

SID: I could fit a whole pack of gum in my—

BRIT: Me too. Me too. Me too!

> *BRIT laughs. SID laughs, mimicking her.*

Do I really sound like that?

SID: Yeah.

BRIT: It sounded stupid.

SID: It's not. You have a good laugh, Brit.

> *BRIT smiles. SID tucks her piece of fabric away.*

> *The light around them widens, revealing what could be a wall of buckets behind them. The GUARD enters humming a song under her breath. SID stares at her. She watches the GUARD with intense precision. She gently, subtly imitates the GUARD's movements.*

> *Then the GUARD sees the flicker of something. Something hidden somewhere on the stage. She puts*

*on a plastic glove and picks it up. It's a knife. She
bags it in a clear plastic evidence bag and exits.*

Down?
BRIT: Up?
SID: Side?
BRIT: DOWN.

Silence.

SID: Want to play?
BRIT: Sure.
SID: Be me or be you?
BRIT: Be me.
SID: I was thinking I want to be her—

SID points at the GUARD.

BRIT: I want you to be me.

Beat.

I like it when you're me.

Beat.

SID: How 'bout I be her being you.
BRIT: Fine. Go.
SID: Wait. I gotta feel it.

SID shakes her head, irritated.

Hi. I came here from Saskatoon, Saskatchewan.
BRIT: The Toon.
SID: Saskatoon—

BRIT: I call it the—
SID: I'm her being you.
BRIT: Right.

Sorry, go on.
SID: so one day I was walking down the street—right—
BRIT: Right—
SID: And I was high.
BRIT: No.
SID: You weren't.
BRIT: I was but I wouldn't say it like that.
SID: But—
BRIT: SHE wouldn't either.
SID: I was walking—feeling good—you know—
BRIT: Yeah. Feeling good!
SID: Yeah, feeling good, and all of a sudden, WHAM. Someone is yelling at me. And there's this fight.
BRIT: YEAH.
SID: And I get cut by this knife.
BRIT: YEAH.
SID: And I stay around because someone else gets stabbed.
BRIT: Because that's what you do.
SID: And I get arrested.
BRIT: YEAH.
SID: Because I stayed.
BRIT: And they think I stabbed him because my blood is on the knife, even though I clearly got cut from the knife—which was not mine—I stayed because I was worried about the guy who got stabbed—because that's what a person does—they stay . . .
SID: But I didn't do it.
BRIT: No. Stop.
SID: . . . You did do it?
BRIT: Of course not.
SID: THEN WHAT?

BRIT: Nothing. Just forget it . . . Let's stop.
SID: I was just gearing up.
BRIT: I'm sick of this part.
SID: It was going to get good and righteous.
BRIT: I know.
SID: This is the best part, talking about your INJUSTICE.
BRIT: I don't feel like it anymore.

Silence.

Just be her.

BRIT points at the GUARD.

SID: Fuck yes.

SID changes her body.

Okay—so—ya—I was like—

She closes her eyes.

I hate women—they got like—shit everywhere—you know—
it's like—hair clips—bobby pins—fucking scrunchies—pads,
tampons. You know there are always things spilling out of
WOMEN. Pieces of sweater—
BRIT: Pieces of sweaters?
SID: Woman are always shedding—
BRIT: What?
SID: Their hair clogs up the shower.
BRIT: Yeah, but sweaters?
SID: Their clothes too—have attachments that come off—the
fuzzy stuff on sweaters—
BRIT: *(laughs)* You're good at her.

SID: I know. Listen, I know I'm a woman but I'm not a *woman*, you know?

BRIT: Oh I know!

SID: When women come and talk to me, I feel like—I gotta connect—I hate connecting—

BRIT: Yeah, I hate connecting.

SID: Women have needs.

BRIT: Yeah, NEEDS—

SID: You can't just be like "hi" to a woman—

BRIT: Yeah, you gotta say like—"How are you?"—

SID: Yeah. I prefer men—a couple of jokes—

BRIT: —couple of "ha has"—

SID: —couple of "BROS!"—

BRIT: No problem—

SID: I mean, working in prison—

BRIT: —as a "correctional—

SID: —"officer"—men will say some dirty things—

BRIT: Some catcalls—

SID: BITCH, hoe, cunt—

BRIT: But—

SID: It's way better.

BRIT: Yeah—

SID: Way better—

BRIT: —than—

SID: —being needed.

BRIT: And connecting.

SID: I hate guarding women.

The two girls share a fit of laughter. Then pounding is heard. The buckets shake. The girls stop and look down. Silence. Then BRIT whispers.

BRIT: Yeah, I hate being a woman.

SID: NO I don't.

BRIT: Are you her? I was being her. I don't either—

SID: She doesn't either.
BRIT: Okay.
SID: . . . It's complicated.
BRIT: Okay.

*BRIT looks uneasy. The GUARD comes in for another
search. This time she finds a green bean hidden
somewhere on the stage. She bags it and exits.*

*SID changes her stance and speaks with a lot of
shoulder movement.*

SID: I'm not an addict. I told her—straight up—I don't want
to be surprised by what I see written on my file after you
"assess" me. I'm honest with her. I tell her addiction is not
my problem, okay, I LIKE SELLING DRUGS. I like MONEY. If I see
a lot of drugs, I'll sell them. If I'm bored, I'll sell. So keep me
away from drugs and keep me away from boredom. Like if
I'm working at a Tim Hortons, I'll sell drugs. Then I get my
file back and it says I'm an addict that's in denial. I don't
know why I even bother talking about anything to them.

Beat.

BRIT: Wow. Can I just say—wow.
SID: It was okay. I've only seen her once.
BRIT: You really had her shoulders down.
SID: I felt good about the shoulders. Your turn.

Silence. BRIT changes.

BRIT: *(dry, wise, older)* Listen girls—a lot of people say I
don't know how you can handle this so calm, cool, and col-
lected, or hasn't it hit you yet? I say, look it, it's hit me. I
know I'm doing time, but what can I do? Am I going to string

myself up and end it? They'll never get me down to that point. NEVER. I hate green beans and racism and that's about it—the rest I just keep on keep on.

SID: Nice.

BRIT: I'm basically a really happy person. Listen girls—back when they had the death penalty they were really scared about hanging people. But now they're just throw'n us in jail. I'm not saying I'm for the death penalty. But they might as well be throwing my life away 'cause I'm gonna be too old to get married and too old to have kids when I get out. But I'm basically a happy-go-lucky person and very little depresses me.

SID: *(nods)* That was pretty good.
BRIT: Yeah.
SID: Particularly when you said happy-go-lucky. That part really worked.

> *Silence.*

BRIT: Did you think it would be like TV?
SID: Here?
BRIT: Yeah.

SID: I don't remember.

> *Silence.*

> *The GUARD comes in and begins her search. SID sees her and stands up.*

Hi.
GUARD: What are you after?

SID: Nothing, just a hello.

The GUARD *laughs, yeah right.*

GUARD: Okay.

SID *laughs, imitating the* GUARD.

The GUARD *shakes her head.*

SID *shakes her head.*

That's enough.

GUARD *moves away.*

SID *speaks softly to herself:*

SID: What are you after?

SID *walks the length of her pod imitating the exact same walk as the* GUARD. *The* GUARD *sees something hidden somewhere on the stage. A tampon. She bags it and exits.*

BRIT: I need more tampoooooooons.
SID: I know.

Silence.

BRIT: It's really making me panic.
SID: You got an extra pad?
BRIT: No. And I really can't handle not having another tampon right now. Like, it's really making me—
SID: Hey, it's okay—

BRIT: No. Like, I've been wearing it for like ten hours and I really can't handle not having another tampon—
SID: I'll try and get you another one.
BRIT: I'm really—
SID: I know.

Silence.

BRIT: Really, I can't handle this.
SID: I'm going to try, on the next round.
BRIT: 'Cause I'm picturing it and—
SID: Shhh. It's okay—
BRIT: I can't—I can't—

SID changes.

SID: I hate jam. It's gooey and stupid.

BRIT takes a deep breath and tries to listen.

But now, I miss jam. I miss having the option; I mean every morning I think about jam—how . . . stupid is that?—
BRIT: I really need a new tampon. I can't stop picturing—
SID: I know.

BRIT starts moaning.

FUCKING HELL. Hello. We need a tampon. HELLO!

SID sees the GUARD.

She needs another tampon. Yes. She does—

GUARD: You think this is a hotel?

SID: Please.

GUARD: You think you can make demands?

SID: She needs it.

GUARD: Don't talk / back—

SID: I'm not talking back. She needs another tampon. Please—

GUARD: In what world is this / my problem?

SID: Why are you being an asshole?

GUARD: Careful.

SID: FUCK YOU.

> *The GUARD grabs her.*

Fuck. Ouch. You're hurting me now. NO. NO. NO. Don't! Just give her.

> *SID spits in the GUARD's face.*

BRIT: NO!

> *The GUARD takes SID away. BRIT sits alone. Time passes; she waits. BRIT closes her eyes. The GUARD begins her search, and finds a calculator hidden somewhere on the stage. She bags it, but then sees something else, a soother. She bags it as well and exits.*

A fragile SID comes back into the pod and sits. BRIT opens her eyes and listens.

. . . Hello.
SID: . . . Hey.
BRIT: . . . Play?
SID: I'm not in the mood
BRIT: . . . Then what?
SID: Then nothing.
BRIT: What's wrong?

Silence. SID takes her knees to her chest.

SID: I don't think I'm going to—
BRIT: You will.
SID: No.
BRIT: You will.
SID: No. When I close my eyes. It's getting worse.
BRIT: It's here.
SID: Here is all there is.
BRIT: No. There's another place.

Silence.

Have you been to minimum?
SID: Yeah. But didn't last long. Something always happens.
BRIT: You go to school?
SID: When they let me.
BRIT: I loved high school
SID: That's disgusting.
BRIT: I did. I really liked math.
SID: That's actually insane.

BRIT shrugs. Silence.

I remember liking grade school. I remember having dirty hands.

BRIT: Dirty hands??? Ooooh SEXY.

SID: No, touching metal fences and monkey bars, you just liked to touch everything in grade school. I remember the feeling of that. It was gross but it was normal.

BRIT: My hands always feel dirty here too.

SID: Priss—

BRIT: I'm not a priss—

SID: Prissy.

BRIT: I'm not prissy.

SID: You are prissy.

BRIT: I care about hygiene.

SID: And math.

BRIT: And math. SO?

Beat.

What were you like in high school?

SID: What are we even talking about?

BRIT: We're just talking about life.

SID: It's boring.

BRIT: Okay. Sorry.

Silence.

SID: When I come home my daughter makes me tea. I know I shouldn't let her but when I come home she studies me to see what kind of mood I'm in and I don't like it, so I let her go make me tea. Then she comes back and we put on one of our favorite mystery shows and I get my good mood back.

BRIT: What's that?

SID: Her.

BRIT: The screw? The screw that . . .

SID nods.

It sounds weird.

SID: I'm trying something different. WE have to EVOLVE, YOU KNOW.

BRIT: She's the screw that put you in seg.
SID: Yeah, I know, but . . . I like her.
BRIT: Like a crush?
SID: No.
BRIT: You have a crush on a screw!
SID: No, I'm not like you—
BRIT: What does that mean?
SID: It means I'm not like you. I don't like girls.
BRIT: You like boys.
SID: No.
BRIT: Then what—
SID: Nothing, I don't like PEOPLE.
BRIT: But you like this screw.
SID: Yeah I do.
BRIT: Why?
SID: She reminds me . . . of something.
BRIT: What?
SID: It's none of your business.

Silence.

BRIT: So you really don't like anyone.
SID: Not like that.
BRIT: Why?
SID: I don't know, I just never have.

Beat.

BRIT: Do you masturbate?
SID: Yeah.
BRIT: So what do you think about?
SID: Gross.

Silence

I guess I think about the feeling of . . .
BRIT: Yes . . .
SID: Coming.
BRIT: Coming?
SID: . . . yeah.
BRIT: That's it.
SID: That's a lot.

Silence.

What do you think about?
BRIT: Boobs. Mostly.
SID: Did you always . . .
BRIT: No . . . When I was in grade eight I had some
boyfriends. I would think about them, but they were all fuzzy
in my head. Like I never thought about them up close. But
then it made me feel self-conscious to have them with me
while I was coming, even just in my head.
SID: That's how I feel. I don't want anyone else there.
BRIT: I want boobs there. I want lots of boobs there.

They laugh.

Silence.

SID: I don't really like talking about this stuff.
BRIT: Okay. I'm sorry.
SID: . . . It's okay. I just don't want to do it again.

BRIT nods.

BRIT: You want to play the game?
SID: Yeah!

BRIT: When I come, no joke, like the moment I come, I picture myself as a man. This is the kind of man I am: baseball cap turned backwards and giant hose between my legs being unleashed. YA. LEAFS. YA. FUCKING. RAPTORS. YA! And everyone's soaked. That's what I think about, at like the peak of my orgasm.

SID: Wow, who's that?
BRIT: *(laughs)* I made it up.

SID: That's not the game.
BRIT: Sometimes I think about that too when I—
SID: But it's not you doing you.
BRIT: It's like me and some made up stuff.
SID: That's not the game.
BRIT: It could be.
SID: It's not.

> *BRIT shrugs and picks up a notebook, opens it, and writes.*

What are you doing?
BRIT: I'm writing.
SID: . . . Why?
BRIT: I'm keeping track of everything that's happening in here.
SID: With me?
BRIT: No. With the screws and stuff.
SID: Why?
BRIT: I dunno. It makes me feel better.

Beat.

SID: It's weird.

BRIT shrugs and goes back to writing.

BRIT: . . . While you were in solitary . . . the baby killer, she—
SID: Yeah. I heard.
BRIT: I feel bad for her.
SID: She was a baby killer—
BRIT: I know, but still—
SID: Still what? You hate them like I do.
BRIT: I know but. She cried every night.
SID: I don't feel bad. I have only so much I can feel bad about and I don't want to feel bad about that.

BRIT goes back to writing in her notebook.

BRIT: Okay, but I do.

The sound of BRIT's writing irritates SID and she gets up to change her shirt. The GUARD, from a distance, watches her.

GUARD: Your breasts offend me.
SID: What? I'm just changing. I'm allowed to change.
GUARD: And your breasts offend me.
SID: Whatever.
GUARD: Put your shirt on. Put it ON. This isn't a club. Where do you think you are?
SID: I was only changing.
GUARD: I don't want to see your breasts again.
SID: I have nowhere else to change.
GUARD: I don't want to see your breasts.
SID: SHUT UP.

GUARD: Thank you. Now I can write you up.

The GUARD leaves. SID looks angry and then smiles.

SID: Your breasts offend me. Your breasts offend me.

BRIT watches SID, then shakes her head. She turns fully away fully from SID. SID pulls out her piece of fabric and rubs it between her fingers. Time passes.

BRIT: I wanna tell you something.
SID: GO.
BRIT: I feel nervous.

SID: . . . Is it about your girlfriend?
BRIT: How do you know?
SID: Come on.
BRIT: What?
SID: You guys are always canoodling.
BRIT: Canoodling?
SID: Touching.
BRIT: Who says canoodling? That sounds like a grandma. And we aren't always touching.
SID: Well you're giggling all the time.
BRIT: I really like her.
SID: No shit.
BRIT: Are you mad?
SID: Mad?
BRIT: Mad.
SID: Why would I be mad?
BRIT: I don't know, because, maybe, well we're close—
SID: We're friends.
BRIT: I know.
SID: I'm not jealous of your girlfriend.
BRIT: Okay.

SID: Okay.

But I don't want to hear about her all the time. Because I find hearing about romance pretty barf-inducing and I don't like wanna analyze anything.

BRIT: Okay.

SID: Like I hate people who analyze texts. There was this girl in grade nine and she was always like, "He texted 'Hey.' WAD DOES IT MEAN?" That shit bores me.
BRIT: We can't text in here—
SID: It was an example.
BRIT: I get it.
SID: Okay.

BRIT: . . . Can I just tell you a few things? Please.

SID: Fine.
BRIT: She said. She said—the sweetest, she was like, "Girl, when you smile I see sunshine."

Beat.

Isn't that sweet. I keep thinking about that.
SID: That's nice. BUT WAIT! Were you outside on the grounds? I mean, was there sunshine?
BRIT: No.
SID: Okay. Cute then. Let's PLLLLLAY.
BRIT: Wait not yet. I wanna tell you something else.
SID: Fine.
BRIT: We kissed.

Beat.

In the shower.
SID: Hey, be careful.
BRIT: It's fine.
SID: No, it's—you can get in a lot . . . You can get moved.
BRIT: It's fine. No one saw. Plus anyway, lots of people—
SID: Get in trouble. I've been a lot of places.
BRIT: Here isn't as bad.
SID: I've seen people put in seg 'cause they were—
BRIT: It's fine—
SID: It's illegal here. You know that, right.
BRIT: We're careful.
SID: I'd think about whether it's worth it.
BRIT: It is. She makes me feel like I'm not here.

Silence. SID *contorts. She's wounded.*

SID: I've seen her fuck other girls.
BRIT: What? When?
SID: Around.
BRIT: When?
SID: I don't know exactly. But I think she's a little—you know.
BRIT: No. I don't know.
SID: She's old enough to be your mom.
BRIT: She's twelve years older than me. Who did you see her with?

Silence.

She's never going to replace you. You're my best friend.
SID: I'm really not worried about it.
BRIT: Who did you see her kiss?
SID: I don't remember.
BRIT: Well if you remember let me know, okay?
SID: Fine.

*Neither girl looks at each other. SID sees the GUARD
coming and stands up. BRIT watches her, irritated. SID
calls after the GUARD.*

Hey! Hey.
BRIT: What are you doing?

SID ignores BRIT. She calls at the GUARD.

SID: Hey. You have a daughter.
GUARD: That is none of your business.
SID: I'm sorry I spat in your face. I'm sorry about that I
was mad.
GUARD: I don't care how you feel.
SID: I'm trying to apologize.
GUARD: I'm glad you realize that what you did won't be
tolerated.
SID: I like the way you walk.
GUARD: You're not going to get far with me. Inmate.
SID: Why do you call me that? The others call me by
my name.
GUARD: A name is a luxury.
SID: A name is a luxury.
GUARD: You caught the loons today, inmate?
SID: Do you live in an apartment?
GUARD: This isn't an interview.

SID laughs.

Laugh away. Watch it, inmate.
SID: WATCH IT, INMATE. You're a fake.
GUARD: What did you say?

SID: You're a fake.

The GUARD *grabs her.* SID *pushes back.*

GUARD: You know how this ends.

The GUARD *takes* SID *away.* BRIT *watches.*

Time passes.

The GUARD *comes in for her search. She finds a stuffed Minnie Mouse, bags it, and exits.*

SID *comes back from segregation. She looks physically weaker, but her energy is manic.*

SID: Hey!
BRIT: Hey.
SID: How are you?
BRIT: Good . . . How are you doing?

SID *nods.*

SID: How are things with your girl?
BRIT: Are you sure you want to talk about it.
SID: I'm asking!
BRIT: They're really good. I feel—I mean she's amazing— Oh god—I can't even tell you—
SID: You can't get a sentence out.
BRIT: It's great.
SID: What do you talk about?
BRIT: Each other.
SID: You just talk about each other?
BRIT: How we feel—
SID: Oh gawd—
BRIT: About each other and about us together
SID: Barf-o-rini.

BRIT: Yeah. You'd hate it.

SID: I'm glad you're, you know, all barfy happy whatever.
BRIT: Thank you. I'm sorry you went to seg again.

Silence.

It's not all happy times, with her.
SID: Well we're not in Disneyland.
BRIT: I know, I just mean. Her husband abused her really
badly. It makes me really angry. She got fifteen years when it
was basically self-defence. It's been ten and now she's up for
parole and I was thinking, maybe, my lawyer could . . .
SID: Could what?
BRIT: Well I have access to better—
SID: Could what?
BRIT: Help her.

SID snorts.

Things happened to her. Her husband did very bad things.
She fought back. It's not fair.
SID: WAAA.
BRIT: It isn't—
SID: Do you two just talk about how good and innocent you
both are together all the time.
BRIT: No, it's not like that, I'm trying to—
SID: BLAH BLAH.
BRIT: Okay. Whatever.

Silence.

What did you do to get here?
SID: Don't ask me. That.
BRIT: I just—

SID: Don't. What's wrong with you? That's MINE to tell.
BRIT: But you never do.

Silence.

. . . Have you ever been to Disneyland?
SID: No. Have you?
BRIT: No.
SID: Well maybe it's just like here then.

BRIT laughs.

BRIT: I'm picturing all the screws dressed up like giant Minnie
Mouses. Like going around counting us dressed with giant
mouse heads.
SID: Yeah and we're like all the princesses.
BRIT: Yeah.

*SID and BRIT laugh. The GUARD enters, this time to do
body searches. SID and BRIT stop laughing and stand
up. The GUARD frisks BRIT first. Silence. Then SID.*

SID: How long have you been here?
GUARD: Long enough.
SID: Why?
GUARD: Building memories.

SID laughs.

SID: I bet.
GUARD: I'm here to build you some memories.

*SID laughs again. The GUARD laughs with her and then
walks away.*

BRIT: What are you doing with her?
SID: Nothing. Just talking.
BRIT: I don't like it.
SID: Then don't watch.

*The two girls stare at each other intensely. Then
look away.*

Time passes.

*The GUARD comes in for her search but this time
she knows exactly where she is looking. She finds
a baggy of white small rocks hidden somewhere on
stage; she shakes her head and exits.*

I'm sorry.

Silence. BRIT writes furiously in her notebook.

I'm sorry, Brit.

BRIT: I want to put a fucking pencil through her eye.

SID laughs.

What?
SID: A pencil—I don't know—it's just—
BRIT: Don't.
SID: Sorry.
BRIT: I'm not in the mood.
SID: *(thinks quickly)* FUCK HER.
BRIT: Yeah.
SID: SHE HAS A FACE OF DICKS!

BRIT: FUCKER FUCKER FUCKER DIE. I just know that fucking screw planted the drugs. She's been clean forever. I would know. I'm going to report it.
SID: Yeah right—
BRIT: I will.
SID: Yeah right it will do anything—
BRIT: I'm on good behaviour—
SID: What does that mean?
BRIT: Nothing. I just, I want to be able to talk to the warden.
SID: She's not going to let you protect your girlfriend.
BRIT: My fiancée. She's my fiancée now.
SID: *(flat)* Congratulations.

Silence.

BRIT: She has a daughter.
SID: Who?
BRIT: My fiancée. And she got her parole.

SID's *whole body changes.*

SID: What?
BRIT: Yeah, she found out last week. She's going to minimum, then she's—she was going to be OUT in two days . . . Now.
SID: . . . I didn't know.
BRIT: So this is seriously fucked, okay?

SID: I'm sorry. I didn't know. I didn't know she had a daughter.

Silence.

I know you're sad. Let's play.
BRIT: I don't want to.

Silence.

SID: . . . I could play her.

BRIT: What the fuck, no. That's sick—

SID: I—

BRIT: This isn't some game. My partner has gone to seg!

SID: I know.

BRIT: No you don't.

SID: I do. I've been. A lot. Have you?

BRIT: She's not like you.

SID: What does that mean?

BRIT: Nothing. I just don't want to play some creepy game about it.

SID: Sorry, okay, I thought it would help.

BRIT: Because everything is a game to you.

SID: No.

BRIT: Because you can't be yourself—

SID: Stop it—

BRIT: so it's either playing this game or howling like a fucking animal. You know they treat you like an animal: because you act like one.

SID: Stop, you're upset but you're being—

BRIT: The warden is going to listen to me because I act like a person. I ACT LIKE A PERSON.

SID: Oh yeah right—with your notebook of all the bad things—haha—your spooky notebook—

BRIT: You'll see, they'll listen.

SID: *(laughs)* Oh yes because *(imitating BRIT)* I'm just an innocent—I'm so innocent—I'm not supposed to be here—

BRIT: I am innocent—

SID: NO ONE CARES.

BRIT: FUCK YOU!

SID: Maybe your girlfriend was getting high because she was sick of screwing you!

BRIT: I'm going to kill you—

SID: With a pencil?

The GUARD comes in. BRIT points.

BRIT: She's provoking me!

SID starts barking like a dog. The GUARD approaches.

GUARD: That's enough.

SID keeps barking.

Why do you make me do this?

The GUARD grabs SID. SID makes biting actions towards The GUARD.

BRIT: No, don't! Sid, stop it!

SID continues to bark. The GUARD tasers SID. BRIT closes her eyes.

When BRIT opens her eyes, SID is gone. BRIT watches the leak. Time passes.

SID enters. She seems smaller; in her fist is the piece of fabric, all balled up.

Hey.
SID: Hey.

Silence.

BRIT: I'm sorry.
SID: Yeah, me too.

Silence.

BRIT: It feels bottomless.
SID: What?
BRIT: My sad.
SID: Yeah.
BRIT: It goes on and on. I remember those really grey days, rain on fall leaves.
SID: Yeah.
BRIT: That used to make me so sad. Now I feel like I am one, a wet leaf.

SID laughs

It's not funny.
SID: . . . Sorry. I thought, I thought it was like poetry.

SID contorts her body to be a wet leaf.

BRIT: I'm going to be moved to minimum.
SID: That's great.
BRIT: Yeah, I guess.
SID: I'm sure she'll join you there soon.
BRIT: Yeah, but I'm going to miss you. A lot.
SID: You shouldn't. Minimum is a lot better; you'll have a kitchen and stuff.
BRIT: Yeah. We'll see each other soon.
SID: Maybe.
BRIT: Are you still mad at me for calling you out.
SID: No, I shouldn't have said. Anyway, I wasn't that mad.
BRIT: Seriously—
SID: I was so pissed. But . . .
BRIT: Yeah . . .
SID: But I don't know—you're my friend and . . . what do you want me to say.

BRIT: You love me?
SID: Barf.
BRIT: You do.
SID: GROSS.
BRIT: Be me.
SID: Okay. I love you. You're my best friend. I'm innocent and good.
BRIT: Yep that's about right.

Silence.

SID: That must be awful.
BRIT: What?
SID: Being good and being here. I know I tease you about it but . . . I can't imagine it. At least I'm bad.
BRIT: You're not bad you just made a bad choice.

SID laughs.

SID: I'm bad. I've always known it. Deep down. I'm a bad guy.
BRIT: You're not bad.
SID: Stop.
BRIT: You're not.
SID: STOP, I AM.
BRIT: I'll be you.
SID: No—
BRIT: SURE, I act out a lot—
SID: You're not good at it.
BRIT: I act out because I care. And it's hard to care. It's hard to feel so many opposing things at once. That's what compassion is. It hurts. It makes you into a wet leaf. I lash out to feel less.
SID: Stop.
BRIT: And then I get in trouble, which makes me feel safe because then I can feel a little less. Feeling bad is easier.

SID: It isn't.

BRIT: Because it's not true. And I can hide.

SID: I'm not good.

BRIT: Sid, you are. That first day, when you got transferred here, do you remember? When I asked you what you liked. You said gum and giraffes. And you didn't like tights.

BRIT smiles, remembering.

And my heart knew.

SID: No—

BRIT: You're my best friend.

SID: No. Brit, you don't know. You don't know what I have done. You don't know who I am.

BRIT: SO TELL ME.

Silence.

Be you.

SID: I am me.

BRIT: No. Be you. Tell me how you got here.

SID: I don't.

BRIT: Please. It's my last day. Do you.

SID: I used to be tall.

BRIT: Really?

SID: Yeah. I was tall for my age and then all of a sudden I got short. Everyone outgrew me. I think it set me up for a life of disappointment. I was never normal. Boo hoo.

SID makes fake crying sounds.

BRIT: . . . How did you get in here?

SID: So boring.

BRIT: Please. Do you.

SID: NO.

BRIT: Fine. Then do her *(points at the GUARD)* doing you.

Silence. SID watches the GUARD in the distance. She speaks from a distance until she doesn't.

SID: Well I guess she would say it all started when she found out her mother wasn't her mother. She was thirteen and then things got . . . she got really obsessed with protecting people who didn't really need it. Once she thought this gym teacher at her school was being inappropriate with a student and she called him on it and he flipped and she hit him. I don't know. It felt so fucking good. And then she did it more.

Silence.

Once her mom knew that she knew. Her mom was different too. Something broke inside of her. Not love but something else. It was the hardest with her dad. He and his new family moved further away and he'd try but that was what hurt, every time he saw her it felt like trying . . . When I started getting violent my mom couldn't handle it and sent me to see someone and I hated that. They gave me some drugs, which made me feel thick, so I stopped and tried some other types of drugs. I don't really like drugs but it just felt like something I should do because I was like a bad kid—I was, like a good kid, and then I was a, like, bad kid. Like being tall and being short.

BRIT: Yeah.

SID: So now I smoke and I'm into drugs, pot mostly, but I hang out with people who are addicted to the harder ones 'cause they're, like, sad. So one time this newbie dealer tries to stiff a friend of mine. Every dealer I ever met was super chill, super nice, but this punk, turns out to be like the older brother of a dealer who wants to make some extra cash to go drinking and be an asshole I guess. So he's wearing a pleather jacket and selling smack to my friend behind a KFC. He says my friend needs to pay double his usual—which was bullshit. My friend was like this timid guy who's clearly fucked up and this douche one-time dealer starts demanding more cash and my friend's desperate, jonzing, and douche is poking him, "Pay up, pay up, bra." Like he's some kinda gangster in a pleather jacket outside a fucking KFC. I mean give me a break. So I gave him my own bucket of fuck it.

BRIT laughs. That energizes SID.

And I scratch his face. And his parents freak out, turns out he goes to private school, and I end up in juvs. And then the first week I get out and I'm on this bus and these dudes are making really stupid jokes to this girl and she's kinda laughing. But you come in here and you see, like, a lot of girls who got fucked up by stuff done to them so I was like, to the girl, "Everything okay?" and she turns red and is like. "Yeah totally." And then I'm about to get off the bus and the guy is like, "Don't worry, we're only going to rape her a little bit." And I did more than scratch him up. Apparently I ended his hockey career. Which I think is awesome. But the girl testified against me. And then I'm here, and the screws in here, they shouldn't be allowed to do what they do, but I just get more and more time. So fuck it. To pieces you know.

BRIT: You're like Robin Hood.
SID: No. I'm not. I like hurting people.
BRIT: You're like Dexter.

Silence.

SID: When I tie up it's because of this feeling. Like this secret inside me. I like hurting people. I like it. And so I tie up because I don't want to feel that way. I don't even want to die; I just want to feel like I'm worth it or something.

BRIT: You are worth it.

SID: I'm a bad guy.
BRIT: No, you're not. You're really not.

SID's body changes.

SID: I put the drugs in your girlfriend's pod. I'm not a wet leaf. I'm a rat. I told on her to the screw. 'Cause I'm bad.

Beat.

I hated her. Because I'm a bad guy.

Silence. BRIT cries.

I don't know why you chose me. Everyone pretends to be innocent but you actually are and . . .

BRIT covers her face with her hands.

You were leaving me. And I wanted to hurt her. I didn't know she had a daughter. I'm sorry. If I'd known she had a daughter.

The GUARD comes to collect BRIT.

GUARD: Are you ready?

BRIT: Yes. Get me out of this hellhole.

SID: I'm sorry. Please. Please!

BRIT doesn't look at SID as she picks up her notebook and leaves.

No!

SID reaches out her hand towards BRIT but she is gone. SID is alone with the GUARD. They stare at each other.

I had a bad dream.

SID pulls out a balled up piece of fabric and unravels it. It is long and almost rope-like now. The GUARD begins to walk away.

Don't go. I'm going to tie up. Please don't leave me alone. No. No. I'm going to tie up.

The GUARD exits. SID is alone.

No. NOOOOOOOO!

She begins to play the game by herself. Being both the GUARD and herself. The leak from the ceiling intensifies.

Don't talk back to me.
Don't touch me.
You don't get to make demands.
I woke up with a feeling.

Don't try this crazy shit with me. I know all about you—I
don't have sympathy for loons.
I don't want trouble.
Good. Stop moving.
I don't like the way you are holding me.
Stop moving.
Calm down.
Breathing feeling sick breathing.
Calm down.
I know you.
I can assure you, you don't. Stop moving.

Lights begin to fade so slowly on SID.

Breathe.

She breathes out.

She holds her breath. The GUARD *walks back in—*

Breathe.
Breathe.
Spit.
Why?
Why not.
You have a daughter?
You want to go to seg?
I don't care.
Care.
Breathe.

SID *spits.*

Breathe.

Spits.

CARE!
You be me.
I'll be you.
You animal.
You. You. Lock her up.
I had a dream.
There's a picture.
I was tall.
I can't.

> *The leak stops dripping. The* GUARD *watches* SID'S *face, dimly lit, and looks into her eyes.*

Do you remember me?

> *The* GUARD *freezes.* SID *disappears in darkness. Then the* GUARD *rushes towards her but trips on the bucket. It tips over, water spilling out, along with a large, wet red leaf.*

> *The* GUARD *picks up the bucket. The leak from the roof begins again. The* GUARD *places the bucket under the leak and looks out at the audience.*

> *Blackout.*

TWO

In darkness. The sound of water dripping intensifies then stops.

Lights up on KIT. She stands naked under a shower that could be made of a bucket or buckets. She is lathering herself up with a bar of Ivory soap. She smiles at us—

KIT: Hi.

Beat.

I'm glad you're here. Let's have some fun!

She looks at the soap and smiles.

There's a line. A line I don't remember. It goes like . . . No. There's this line you can cross. That's right. I remember now. There's this line that you get cut off at. No. Go back to the end of the line. Back to the first line. You're on one side or another. That's it. That's the line. The line between sanity and insanity. The line between alive and dead. Well, actually there're two lines it seems, alive, no breath, and death. There's a line between poor and living in poverty. Between a downturn and a depression. Between a cold front and sex—no, between a cold front and love—no, scrap that and go back.

Wait.

She looks at her body and the soap, confused. Then remembers. She smiles and continues lathering up.

Sometimes I'd watch a line at a supermarket and think, what's happening here? Okay, I get it, we're coming here for food, food that has been harvested then brought here and organized and priced and then I think, okay, I need food to eat and that's why I am lining up to pay for it. But then I think—wait, what?

She pauses with the soap.

Right.

She goes back to soaping herself and smiles.

Sometimes lining up for a bus makes sense and then sometimes you fall out of—SOMETIMES—I'd kiss my girlfriend and I'd think—this feels good—yes—oh—yes—then—what am I doing pressing my mouth into hers? What is this? Lips. Tongue. Her tongue in mine. What? Sorry. I'm getting confused.

She closes her eyes.

I'm here talking in the shower.

She opens them.

I'm talking to a room of people. Wait, no.

She closes them again.

I'm here. Talking to myself.

She opens them again.

I killed my best friend. I know I absolutely crossed the line there . . . But honestly that's not what worries me. It's all the other lines.

She hears something and puts the soap down. Two correctional officers stand in front of the shower. We can't see their faces.

CO1: It's time.

KIT doesn't move.

MOVE!

She stays still and looks at us.

KIT: You ready? Fun time.

CO1: Okay, fine. You want to play it this way then.

CO1 goes to grab KIT's arm and slips because KIT is so soaped up. KIT starts laughing hysterically. CO2, furious, tries to pin a naked KIT to the ground, but she keeps slipping on her soaped-up body. KIT keeps laughing, leaving both of them on the ground.

KIT: Hi. I believe it is completely insane being a human being and nobody gets away with it fully. A different set of circumstances and you could be me, no problem.

She puts on her clothes as the correctional officers
clean up her mess.

This place was created to be better.
But it slipped.
Just like me.

It tried.
For a little while.
Just like me.

This place was supposed to pave the way for a new way.
Creating choices. Rehab—*(cough)*—ilitation. When it first
opened they had cabins for women to be with their families.
They didn't have a maximum area. The screws didn't wear
uniforms or carry tasers. There were minimal strip searches.
There were scholarships for education. There was room.

KIT sees a toilet, which could be made of a bucket.
She has an idea.

She pulls down her pants, sits on the toilet, and
smiles at us.

Hi.

Beat.

You have to use what you've got. That's life. You use what
you got—never mind if you think you got nothing—'cause
you always got something.

She pulls out a plastic bag, hidden under her leg.

This place started off meaning well. But then . . . Money got cut. And the more money that got cut the further they got from the idea of the place and the further they got from the idea of the place they forgot it.

She puts the plastic bag on her hand.

Just like me. The further I got away from love. I forgot it.

She reaches her hand into the toilet.

The further they got—the more they forgot—and then suddenly all they could see was what was in front of them. Day by day is what they say. It's supposed to help the cravings, but I've learned the hard way how dangerous it is to not see too far ahead.

She fumbles around in the toilet.

The funny—spoiler it's not funny—thing is. I went to prison for possession and intent to sell. I got two years . . . Now I have twenty-five plus.

CO2 knocks on the door. KIT speaks a little quicker.

A lot of people come here for short sentences but then you get in a fight, smoke something you shouldn't, wail a little too loudly, and you get a bigger sentence tacked on and that makes you more depressed and you act out and more gets tacked on. Act out tack on act out tack on act out tack on and on and on.

And then suddenly there are double the women. And the screws start wearing these tough LARGE in CHARGE uniforms—

CO2: Time's up.

KIT pulls her hand out of the toilet and starts talking very quickly.

KIT: And carrying tasers and the nice cottages are crammed full and not nice anymore and suddenly they need a maximum and suddenly it's full of women!

Because no one is leaving. Who cares that this place was designed specifically not to have a maximum.

CO2: You have five seconds.

KIT: This place tried and failed. It's made some bad "choices" just like me. The only difference is—it doesn't seem to get punished.

The stall door is opened.

That's why. I have to use what I got.

KIT smashes a handful of shit into CO2's face. KIT laughs as CO1 grabs her and puts KIT in segregation, then leaves.

The best way to hide something is to let them find something else.

KIT opens her hand, and in it is a razor blade. She winks at us.

Hi.

She takes out a Popsicle stick hidden in the elastic waist of her underwear.

At its core. Prison is all about drugs.
People who do drugs.
People who sell drugs.
And the people who should be on drugs.

We watch as KIT makes a knife using the blade,
Popsicle stick, and pieces of her hair braided together.

My mother named me Kitten. Obviously, I go by Kit.
I never knew my father.
But sometimes I miss them both, like a fever.
Hot from the inside.
My mother sang me beautiful songs.
She loved me but she didn't always choose me.
When I was two she met another man who was very tall.
When I was three she got pregnant again—and had my
sister.
Her name's Lucky—don't get me started—Lucky and Kitten.

I loved my sister but I always thought she looked like a doll.
When she was older she was so good at being a person.

I wasn't.

Our mother died.
Lucky cried.
The tall man didn't know what to do.
I did.
I did drugs.

Once she is finished she hides the knife back in the
elastic waist of her underwear.

The reason I got life in here was because my best friend
asked me to help her kill herself.

Time passes. KIT waits. Her cell door opens and the GUARD from the first section appears.

GUARD: Kit. Let's go.

KIT whips around and looks at the GUARD, surprised.

KIT: You new?

GUARD: To you. Come on, let's go.

KIT gets up and braces, expecting the GUARD to grab her arm hard. The GUARD doesn't. She hums a song and guides her gently back to KIT's pod. Then the GUARD hands her a letter. KIT looks at it suspiciously. Once the GUARD leaves she reads it.

KIT: What. What. What.

She reads through it again to make sure she understands it and then she whispers to herself.

She wants to see me.

She paces around her pod and calls out to the GUARD.

Hey, hey! Excuse me. What do I need to do to get a pen? I know I'm a fucking brat but what would I need to do to get a pen and paper? Tell me?

The GUARD comes up to her.

GUARD: You don't have your writing privileges.

KIT: Look, I'll do anything.

The GUARD smiles.

ANYTHING!

GUARD: Earn them back.

The GUARD leaves. KIT looks at us, but she doesn't say anything. She sits quietly.

KIT: I can't talk to you. I have to be good.

Her legs are shaking. She kisses the letter again and again.

Then, she waits.

Time passes.

The GUARD returns on her rounds, humming softly. KIT smiles sweetly.

Pen? Paper?

The GUARD walks away.

Time passes.

The GUARD returns on her rounds, humming softly.

Hey. Nice tune. Pen?

The GUARD walks away. Time passes.

The GUARD returns on her rounds, humming softly.

Pen?

The GUARD *walks away.* KIT *turns fully away from the audience and waits.*

Time passes.

The GUARD *returns, humming softly.* KIT *gets up and says nothing.* KIT *and the* GUARD *both look each other in the eyes. Then the* GUARD *nods and hands her a pen and paper.* KIT *grabs it quickly.*

Thank you.

The GUARD *smiles and walks away.* KIT *starts writing quickly and roughly but then stops herself. She takes a deep breath and starts again writing carefully and lovingly.*

(to herself) Yes. Yes. Yes.

Once she is done, she hands the letter to the GUARD.

Time passes.

KIT *has combed her hair; she is waiting patiently to be taken to the visitation room. She is excited.*

CO1 *and* CO2 *escort her out of her pod. But they don't lead her to the visitation room; instead, they lead her towards a segregation cell.* KIT *panics, realizing what is happening; she struggles.*

No. What are you doing? I have a visitor. This is a mistake.
You can't. NO! Not today. Not today. I've been really good. For
a month. You can't do this!

*The two correctional officers laugh as they lock KIT in
segregation.*

No, come on. Fuck you. No, I'm sorry, okay. I'll do anything,
not today. Put me in seg for a year. Just not today! PLEASE.

The two correctional officers walk away.

KIT kicks the walls, having a tantrum.

An echo of SID.

*Then KIT stops. She hears something, the GUARD hum-
ming in the distance. KIT thinks, then grabs at her
chest with one hand and with the other hand she
grabs under her shirt.*

I can't breathe. I can't. I'm—I'm having a. Please. Please help
me. I can't. I can't—I can't. Breathe. PLEASE.

*She makes loud choking sounds. The GUARD hears
this. KIT continues to hyperventilate. The GUARD opens
the seg window and sees KIT in distress.*

GUARD: Hey, It's okay. Deep breaths. Deep breaths.

*The GUARD opens the door and moves towards KIT,
who is trying to take deep breaths.*

You're okay.

The GUARD *touches her shoulder.* KIT *pulls something out from her underwear. The sound of dripping water.*

Darkness. We hear the words "Code Yellow" on repeat and then it stops. A light slowly comes up on KIT's *face. She looks out at us and smiles.*

KIT: Hi. I came out talking and I never shut up. That's what my mom always said.

The light comes up fully to reveal that the GUARD *is sitting on a bucket, her arms tied behind her back with her belt.* KIT *is pointing a knife at her neck. She speaks to the* GUARD.

DON'T MOVE.

Then she looks back at us.

I talked myself to sleep and I talked myself awake again.

KIT *looks away from us to something else in the distance.*

NO ONE GETS HURT IF YOU LISTEN TO ME. I HAVE SOME DEMANDS. First, I want a Pepsi and three cigarettes put through here and a LIGHTER. *(points)* That's the first thing. GO.

KIT *comes back to us.*

I learned a lot of shitty things from my mom and nothing from my dad, but I learned how to love from my best friend.

The GUARD *looks around to see who* KIT *is talking to. The* GUARD *can't see us.*

KIT realizes the GUARD is watching her.

DON'T. Don't watch me.

When I first came here the doctor kept asking me if I heard voices. I was like—bitch, please—you think I'd let you guys talk back?

Then she looks at the GUARD.

But seriously.

The GUARD looks down. Satisfied, KIT looks back out at us.

They've made these decisions. About you. And then everything you do is in reaction to the decisions they've made. A prison in a prison in a prison. My two-year-old daughter thought I lived in a prism *(laughs)* like I was some kind of genie. She said, "Mommy's in a prism with rainbows." I don't care where you're from—that's cute as fuck.

KIT sees something.

PUT THEM THERE. YEAH. Step away now. NOW.

Back to us—

She's no longer two. She's no longer my daughter either.

KIT continues holding the knife and reaches with the other hand towards the Pepsi and the cigarettes. She opens the can of Pepsi with one hand and drinks for a long time. Then closes her eyes and whispers like a child. The GUARD watches her.

That's so good.

She opens her eyes and the GUARD *looks quickly away.*

I saw my best friend as soon as she was transferred here. BIG eyes and too much hair. Her hair was so long it made you feel worried. You know. Like she spent too much time growing it.

I was talking in the eating place.
And she answered back.
She just assumed it was all for her.
Ha. Maybe it was.

We talked. We talked about everything except what she did to end up here. I knew. She knew I knew.

KIT lights a cigarette with one hand. She sees something.

DON'T. I will burn her.

She takes the cigarette really close to the GUARD'S *eye.*

STAY BACK. GOOD.

There was this river of sorrow under everything she did and at night she was drowning in it.

(to herself) That's good. Yeah, I like the way that sounds. River of sorrow.

The GUARD *begins shaking.* KIT *tries to look away.*

My best said she'd tried six times. She'd tried and then been put in seg. AND then tried again and was put in seg for longer. She said she couldn't take the isolation so she wouldn't try again until she knew it would work. Didn't take her too seriously until one day we were in the sitting place and she grabbed my hand and said, "I will and should die. We can only go forward if you know that." I looked into her eyes and saw something I have never seen before.

Truth.

> *KIT looks at the* GUARD, *who is now shaking uncontrollably.*

I told my best everything and sometimes it hurt to remember. The more I told her about my mom overdosing the more I saw it from a distance. The doctor here always wants me to go back and FEEL it, but guess what? I LIKE being from a distance.

Please stop shaking.

> *The* GUARD *tries but can't stop. Back to us—*

I can see myself and sometimes I think I'd like to give that girl a hug. My doctor told me—YOU ARE THAT GIRL, but he also only talked to me for ten minutes and decided that I should get transferred to maximum so . . .

> *KIT holds the* GUARD *with both her arms to stop her from shaking, and then she takes her knife and with one arm holds it against the* GUARD'S *throat.*

OKAY. My next demand is— YOU LISTENING, 'CAUSE SHE WILL DIE. REMEMBER, I ALREADY GOT TWENTY-FIVE PLUS. SO HAHA, YOU

FUCKERS. Demand number two: there's a girl, visiting me today. You need to bring her here NOW. She's here in the building. I know it. GET HER. NOW! I just need to talk to her. I'll let this one go if I can just talk to my VISITOR.

KIT speaks to the GUARD.

Hum that song.

The GUARD looks panicked.

That song you always hum when you walk. HUM IT.

The GUARD slowly does. KIT lets go of the GUARD's shoulders. KIT moves around the cell, letting the hum calm her. Then she looks back to us—

When I watched my mom die, something very important, inside of me, disappeared.

Lucky got lucky. She played on the right side of the line. She was young enough, cute enough; she had her dad; she found a home. I eventually found one too, except it was not on the right side. It was anything you could smoke, take, inhale, bump, shoot, yes please more yes I love it come on. COME ON. Put it in me.

Then.
I got pregnant.
Life.

And I stopped. I stopped while I had her inside me.

(angry) I did. I fucking did.

And I loved her. More than I thought there was room for. But there's this other thing. This thing that no one prepares you for. Love didn't make the other pain go away. There's a lot that is unfair about life, but this, this is the single most unfair thing.

Love and pain don't cancel each other out.

> *The GUARD has stopped humming. KIT looks at the GUARD. The GUARD feels her eyes and look at her. KIT speaks to her.*

They should be able to cancel each other out.

> *The GUARD starts shaking again. KIT pauses; she looks really young for a moment and asks the GUARD quietly—*

How long do you think this is going to take?

> *The GUARD is shaking so wildly she can't answer. KIT looks away from the GUARD. KIT looks back out at us.*

I sell drugs 'cause I need money. For my baby. I do what I know how to do. Then. Deal gone wrong. Two years. Eight months on good behaviour. I was allowed to have my daughter come with me. It wasn't easy. More drugs in prison than dealing drugs. But I meet my best and she helps me.

She knew things. Like when my baby cried a lot, I took it personally, but my best—she just picked her up, held her really high above her head, like magic my baby would stop crying. She knew that my baby just wanted to be taller. It's hard to be so tiny.

KIT smiles to herself then looks at the GUARD *and yells—*

STOP FUCKING SHAKING!

The GUARD *stops her body from shaking but her teeth still chatter in shock. Back to us—*

Lucky changes her name to Lucy and meets a really great guy and they come visit us. Lucky Lucy loves my daughter.

My best, she keeps me going. Keeps me clean.

Then she asks me.
For help.

KIT looks at us, then back at the GUARD. *She chooses to speak to the* GUARD.

My best friend asked me to help her end it. End the pain. I didn't want to. But. She said it was the only way out for her because of what she had done. I got her what she needed.

I WAS HELPING HER.

The GUARD *looks at* KIT; *they stare at each other.*

Before she . . . she talked about her kids. She told me that she was supposed to die with them. I'm in trouble. FUCK. Because I helped her.

The GUARD *looks away.* KIT *comes back to us—to calm herself—*

They take my daughter away.

I'm not safe for her.

(very quietly) No.

I get twelve more years. And they say, "What kind of person chooses their best friend over seeing their daughter"—but I didn't choose anything.

We're not working for her anymore. She looks back at the GUARD.

Look at me.

The GUARD *does—terrified.* KIT *speaks to her.*

I didn't know it was a choice, people don't lay out these two options and say choose, it's only after they say you made a choice.

KIT *catches something in the distance.*

Get those people away. You try and shoot me I will TAKE her with me.

She holds the knife back up to the GUARD'S *face.*

Lucky Lucy takes my daughter in full time. It takes two years until I see my daughter. Visitation. I see her and she doesn't know who I am and I wonder.

Lucky Lucy's got this expression on her face.

You're calling her yours, aren't you?

Lucky Lucy denies it. No. Loves her like a daughter but she's not calling her that. And my daughter says.

KIT stops—looks down and speaks to herself.

I don't like it here.

Back to us—

This visit fucks me up and I do some drugs

Back to the GUARD—

OKAY I KNOW BUT

Back to us—

And then I get in a fight. With a guard. I'm mad. I hurt the guard. Crossed that final line. I get twenty-five plus. Game over. Eventually I get to see my sister LUCKY LUCY but she doesn't bring my daughter AND I see what is happening. And I say okay. You take her. She's yours. Because.

To herself—

Because.
I have nothing left.
Except.

Back to the GUARD—

Except.
I guess, for me, the important thing is, I had a daughter.

The GUARD looks into KIT's eyes. Silence. KIT holds her gaze.

GUARD: I have a daughter.
KIT: Don't talk!
GUARD: I love my daughter.
KIT: SHUT UP.
GUARD: I love my daughter.

The GUARD starts to hyperventilate.

KIT: STOP IT. Stop it, okay. Stop. I can't.

KIT speaks quickly, also having trouble breathing. She ignores us now—speaking only to the GUARD.

Listen, I tried to do this your way. I tried to be good for months but then some screw hates me and takes away my visiting privileges. Just 'cause. I tell them my daughter's coming, right. I plead. I beg. But it's not enough. Nothing's enough FOR YOU PEOPLE. She's coming and I have to see her. It's been eleven years and suddenly she writes me—she's calling me her aunt, but I have to tell her the truth because.

GET HER HERE NOW!

It all repeats again. That's what I've learned here, that's the one and only important thing I've learned here.

It repeats.

I have to show them I am serious. I'm sorry but I have to show them.

She's going to stab the GUARD *but then the* GUARD *sees something.*

GUARD: LOOK!

The GUARD *points with her neck.*

KIT *looks out and she sees—it's her visitor. She's there.*

KIT *reaches her hand out towards her daughter. She speaks so softly.*

KIT: My baby.

Blackout. The sound of dripping water becomes louder and louder until it stops.

THREE

Lights up on a girl waiting.

GIRL1: I'm just waiting. I mean, I'm waiting. Sorry—not sorry—my mom told me not to use just, like, well also not like—but my mom said that women use just and like and sorry too much—so it's not good anymore. Bad words. so I'm waiting—I'm ten, in case you were wondering—people often think I'm twelve 'cause I'm tall, which actually is a disadvantage because people expect more from tall people—in my experience, for example, "Can you get that thing from the top shelf?" Short people never have to do that. I mean maybe they have to climb through tiny tunnels, probably, but things on top shelves are way more common than tunnels, in my experience.

I'm waiting for my dad. He's the last, always, for pick up at the after-school program. But he's the absolute best ultimate dad so he can be late. My mom says being the ultimate dad is not an excuse for LEAVING YOUR DAUGHTER TO WAIT. But I have a feeling that my mom never had an ultimate dad, so she doesn't really know the ultimate dad rules.

Another girl enters a different space with a large Christmas wreath in her hand.

GIRL2: It's just this awful moment. When this teacher assistant hands me this wreath, and she's like, "Bring it to your family," and it's in this moment that I have to decide whether I'm going to ignite a truth bomb and explode this moment into a thousand awkward pieces—or just take the wreath. I try—"No thank you, someone else should take it, I don't celebrate." And she's like, "But wreaths aren't Christian, they're about the winter solstice," and I'm like—"It's okay," and she's like, "You deserve this" and "Take this." / And I'm just stuck.

GIRL1: I really don't mind waiting. Because sometimes when parents are late or yell at the wrong times they feel really bad and then they are extra nice. And that extra nice feels extra good. My mom is always on time but she is always grumpy. My dad is always late but he is always smiling. Whenever I talk to my mom about by dad, she gets this stone look. Like she is trying so hard not to have an expression. Which is actually really hard.

 GIRL1 tries to not have an expression.

GIRL2: So I take the wreath and say—I'll wait here for my parents.

GIRL1: Another kid's mom just—not just—picked him up. Yep, she's got the guilty smile, but she also looks grumpy. Grumpy guilt. Grumpy and then guilty about feeling grumpy and then feeling grumpy for feeling guilty.

GIRL2: And I wait for the teacher's assistant to leave.

GIRL1: Now I am officially the LAST kid / waiting.

GIRL2: I pretend to wait for a parent to walk through that door. I can do that face. The waiting face.

She does a face of waiting, GIRL1 *and* GIRL2 *share the same expression for a moment.*

GIRL1: The only thing I don't like about waiting is I just—not JUST—hate the way the after-school teacher / looks at me—

GIRL2: But then the teacher's assistant decides to wait with ME and I realize there is a HUGE problem in my plan. / I DIDN'T THINK THIS THROUGH.

GIRL1: She looks at me like—it must be so HARD FOR / YOU.

GIRL2: I know I should just leave, I'm thirteen—nearly fourteen—but I've made this big production about staying—
GIRL1: She doesn't / understand—
GIRL2: I don't want to / tell her—
GIRL1: The ultimate dad rules—
GIRL1 / GIRL2: What if—
GIRL1: She calls / my mom—
GIRL2: We sit here / for hours.
GIRL1: Come on, Dad!
GIRL2: Just go. So, I'm / waiting.
GIRL1: / I'm just waiting.

Lights up on a third girl in her own space.

GIRL3: I'm not waiting. I want to be clear about that. I have an excellent mother who works really hard, and because of that I've learned to wait for her without "waiting." I don't "wait" for her after school. I take a bus. I text a heart emoji when I leave and a thumbs up when I get home. I don't "wait" for my mother to come home. I do my homework and I make

dinner so that when she does come home I can spend time
with her.

GIRL2: Imaginary waiting is awful because now it looks like
my imaginary parents don't care about me. Better to have no
parents than imaginary parents that don't care, right?

GIRL3: My teacher was like, "Is it hard to have a mother who
works so much?" My teacher's what my mother would call "a
bleeding liberal." I asked her what a bleeding liberal was and
she said, "Someone who tries too hard to be nice and insults
you." I got it. Grade five is full of those. *(imitating a "girly"
girl)* "Nice side ponytail—but maybe it should be more to the
side."

GIRL3 *makes a look of pure hatred.*

GIRL2: I used to have a grandfather. That was / something.

GIRL3: I told the teacher that it was actually great to have a
mother that worked so much because it was a great example of strength and independence. She was like, "Er, I
didn't—um—ah—ah—blah."

Beat.

I'm a very precise but polite person, so I said, "Oh I know
you didn't MEAN to, but perhaps next time you can choose
your language a little more carefully." She turned BLOOD RED—
Haha— / Bleeding liberal.

GIRL2: Everyone at school knows I live in a group home.
Between fosters. Or they know enough not to ask if my
parents are coming. But this teacher's assistant is new.

Caretaker comes in to mop the floor. The teacher's assistant and I go sit on top of a desk.

GIRL1: I SEE / HIM!

GIRL2: Fuck this waiting. Fuck this teacher's / assistant.

GIRL1: The doors open and I see him coming with a big smile. And all the waiting has been worth it. When I hug him.

GIRL3: I make great omelettes—that's just a fact.

GIRL1: I'm SORRY but it's JUST LIKE the best / feeling.

GIRL3: Because I have all this extra / time.

GIRL2: So I look her straight in the / eye.

GIRL1: Seeing him makes it worth it.

GIRL2: And walk over to this bucket filled with dirty water and I throw the wreath in. SMASH IT IN.

She throws the wreath in the bucket.

And I say, "I don't celebrate the FUCKING winter solstice either!" And I look at her face. It scrunches up in shock and anger and she's hurt but it's better than if I had told her the truth: don't have a dad. Mom went to jail for killing him.

Beat.

GIRL3: I feel bad for the other kids at school. They don't know how not to wait.

Time passes.

GIRL1: I'm just—I'm waiting for my boobs to grow. It's so depressing. I went from being really tall to being really short in two years. I did all my growing in grade four and now I'm in grade seven suddenly short and I'm the ONLY one waiting for my boobs to grow. It's just me and this other girl, but she's a gymnast so—IT'S NOT EVEN COMPARABLE! I ask my mom to take me to the Bay to get a bra. She's been so distracted lately—but whatever. My dad barely visits me—but whatever. The saleswomen takes my measurements—she's like, "Nope, it's just baby fat, no need for a bra." SO EMBARRASSING. THEN my mom says, "That's rude, she just has a HEALTHY-looking body." And buys me this sports bra. Now my boobs will look even smaller! We don't talk about it all the way home. I'm DYING till I get to my room and slam the door in my mom's face and put my face into my pillow and scream.

Beat.

. . . Then I hear it. This horrible sound. My mom. Crying. *She's* crying about *my* boobs . . . I know my mom isn't crying about my boobs. I'm not an idiot. My mom cries a lot. Sometimes I think it's because of her family. They messed up. My mom's sister is in prison. My mom's shoulders always go up when we talk about my aunt. She smiles really hard but her shoulders go up. Adults always think we don't notice the small things. But that's basically all we notice. Like how my mom tells me she loves me all the time. It feels too much. My dad only says it when we say goodbye and I know it's true. I know it's true with my mom too but sometimes it feels like she's filling something up that can't be filled.

GIRL3: I'm waiting for my mom's bad mood to pass. Frankly, I'm dreading becoming an adult and getting "moods." It feels like when you're an adult you can just catch them off something as small as the wrong look—bam—bad mood. When my mom comes home from work I make her tea and I say, "A*nother day*?" And she says, "Y*es, another day,*" then she takes the tea and—

Beat.

Smiles at me. Honestly, it's the best moment of my day. Then she has her decompression moment. I count to about thirty, then climb up next to her on the couch. She opens her arms and I snuggle in and we watch our shows. But sometimes she needs more than a decompression moment. She's caught a mood and I have to wait it out. I usually go to the kitchen, because if I am around her and she sees that I see that she has a mood, she REALLY doesn't like it. My mom and I love television—sometimes I think I have two lives. This one and the one we're watching together. We like to watch British mystery shows mostly. My mom sees lots of hard things and they go into her. That's why she needs to decompress.

GIRL2: I'm waiting to find out where my mom got transferred. It's fucking ridiculous. She was supposed to stay in Winnipeg—WINNERPEG—she was supposed to stay near me but now I think she's been transferred to Kitchener. I mean, where even the fuck is that? So I find out it's in Ontario. Disgusting. Now I'll have to take a plane to see my mom— with what money? Mom says she can work there, but I looked it up—$6.95 a day is not going to get me a plane ticket. It'll all be the same anyway. Going there, getting there, forms, metal detectors, patted, searched, dog-smelled, all to sit at those horrible tables and spend twenty-five minutes with Mom, where she'll probably say something like, "I miss you and I miss jam. I still miss having jam, isn't that strange?" And I'll be like, "Okay." I was seven when my mom went to prison. I went to live with my grandfather. When Mom got her sentencing my grandfather took me to see it 'cause that's what he thought he was supposed to do. When the judge said fifteen years, possible parole in ten, my mom collapsed and reached her arm out to me like this—

She demonstrates.

At first, everyone would give me sweets. No matter where I was someone would give me chocolate. I learned that's what people do when something bad happens. They give you sugar. My grandfather didn't say a lot but every night before bed he'd tell me, "It's going to get better, kiddo." I miss him . . . I'm sixteen, almost seventeen now . . . My mom got put into seg right before she was transferred. She said she can never go to seg again—it will kill her. I said, you want to make me an orphan? That shut her up. I could tell she was going to cry but sometimes you have to ignore your mother's emotions . . . Sometimes I worry that the only reason I'm waiting for my mom to get out is because I think I'm supposed too.

> *Time passes.* GIRL1 *holds a picture. We hear the words "Code Yellow" repeat on a loudspeaker.* GIRL1 *looks around the room she's in.*

GIRL1: I'm just waiting. I don't care about "justs" or "likes" anymore; it's another way for the patriarchy to police my voice. I told my mom that and she got SILENT.

> GIRL2 *paces the perimeter of another room that she's in.*

GIRL2: I'm waiting to see my mom. I have something I need to say to her.

GIRL1: I'm here to see my aunt. Apparently I came here when I was three but didn't like the way it smelled and then refused to come back. I didn't tell my mom. I found out how to write to my aunt and I asked her, "Can I see you?" I didn't hear anything, gave up, BUT THEN I got a letter back with a time and some information about all the stuff I have to do. Got a fake ID, said I was eighteen instead of thirteen, hopped on a bus, and came here.

GIRL2: But when I got here a guard said code purple to another guard and put me in this room by myself. Which isn't / normal.

GIRL1: I got here and was searched. Pretty awful. Starting to understand why my mom doesn't come here. Then they asked me to wait in this room. There's a giant kennel but no dog. I'm thinking about where the dog is.

GIRL2: I haven't seen my mom since she got transferred here. We had a really good feeling that she'd get her parole, so we thought we'd just wait it out—save the money. I got a job as a hostess and as soon as I found out Mom got her parole I bought her a present. This set of jams, like all different kinds, like maple pomegranate and stuff. I was nervous. I had something I wanted to tell her in person. But two days before she was going to be released, she got caught with crack cocaine. Straight to segregation . . . Luckily I kept the receipt for the jam so.

> GIRL3 *enters the same room as* GIRL1, *holding a chocolate bar and looking nervous.*

GIRL3: I'm waiting for my mom's shift to end.

GIRL1: I've come for answers.

GIRL3: Every Tuesday I take the bus to this museum where there's an after-school program for kids. I'm thirteen now, so I'm basically volunteering my time to babysit. My mom picks me up at 5:30. It's the only day of the week my mom finishes early enough to drive me home, so it's special. But today my mom didn't come. A man picked me up, said nothing about what was going on, and put me in this room with another girl, who looks really stressed out.

GIRL3 sits next to GIRL1 and smiles politely; GIRL1 gives a strange expression back.

GIRL1: They just brought another girl here. I want to smile at her, but I can't seem to.

GIRL3: I don't know what this other girl is trying to communicate to me, but her expressions are very strange.

GIRL1: This building feels like high school / but worse.

GIRL3: My mom's shift was supposed to end over an hour ago. Everybody's being really nice. A little too nice. And I heard them say, "Don't put her in there," and then, "Well, we need everyone we can—it doesn't matter." This was obviously concerning.

GIRL1: It's too bright in here. My mom is all about good lighting. It's pretty dark in my house, made my dad angry back then—he said he could never find his matching socks—no overhead light—I'm pretty sure that's why they got divorced.

She laughs nervously.

I'm lying. Okay. I'm feeling uneasy in this room and it's reminding me of all the times I've felt uneasy and that makes me want to lie. The real reason my parents got divorced as far as I can tell had to do with this one fight. I heard my dad say, "I can't keep lying." And my mom dropped something and it broke and she said, "Don't you love her?" And he said, "Of course, how dare you ask me that?" And there was dead silence.

GIRL2: I didn't hear anything from mom till a week ago. She calls me panicked and says, "The drugs were planted!" But honestly, I don't know what to believe. She also informs me that she's engaged to her girlfriend. Bye bye parole and hello—stepmother? I'm like, okay, but mom, I have something to tell you; I'm pregnant.

GIRL1: I don't like that empty kennel.

GIRL3: A correctional officer gave me this chocolate bar. I've been here like a hundred times and I have never been given FREE chocolate.

GIRL1: I'd feel better if there was a dog in there—even if it was a scary dog I'd feel better. And that girl with her / chocolate.

GIRL3: I wish this girl would stop staring at me. I guess she's wondering why I'm not eating this / chocolate bar.

GIRL1: I don't know why they didn't give me a chocolate bar—that's just rude.

GIRL3: I guess I should eat it

> GIRL3 *eats it really quickly.* GIRL1 *watches her with awe.*

That was probably too quickly.

GIRL1: Well, maybe she's diabetic.

> GIRL3 *scrunches up the wrapper angrily and throws it into a bucket.*

GIRL2: Yep, I got pregnant. I keep wanting to say I caught pregnant. I feel like the withdrawal method worked on everyone except me. But I have bad luck. My youth counsellor is like—"Luck is about choices." "Choices" is the big word right now. Your mother made bad "choices." I think having your mom kill your dad is pretty fucking bad luck but whatever. Choices.

GIRL3: My mother works with criminals, who are actually women who have made bad choices; she really tries to help them.

GIRL2: Mom got super quiet when I told her. All I could hear was her breathing on the other end of the phone. Then she said, "No. It has to stop somewhere."

GIRL1: Now my dad always looks guilty and I'm starting to forget the other way he used to look at me and my mom keeps saying I love you like she wants to drown me in it.

> GIRL1 *quietly starts to cry.* GIRL3 *looks at her.*

GIRL3: It's going to be okay.

GIRL1: Yeah um, I know. I'm just waiting.

GIRL2: It's all a POLLOCK. That painter—you know—A MESS. That's how I remember my childhood. Nothing up close. I

said that to my counsellor and she looked so impressed. I
was like—"Don't look so fucking impressed that I know who
Pollock is." I want to have it. And everyone is, "No, don't BE
STUPID. And I'm like—CHOICES. At first, I was like—obviously
I'm going to abort. But now it feels nice in here—

She touches her belly.

Except for the barfing. And I don't want that feeling to go
away. My mom told me I had to come see her. NOW. I'm
like, with what money? But it turns out my mom's fiancée Britton's parents are loaded, and they pay for my plane
ticket.

GIRL1: I have this gut feeling. Almost like a memory. But out
of focus. Like in spots. Plus I found this picture.

GIRL2: *(touching her belly)* I take my first plane. Up in the
sky I realize I know what I have to tell my mom when I see
her. But now I'm stuck here waiting! I really need to see
my mom.

GIRL3: My father played the cello. He died before I was born.
My mom rarely talks about him, but she does hum this one
song under her breath when she's cleaning. Sometimes it's
like she doesn't even realize she's doing it. I asked her about
it and she said my father wrote it for her . . . I really need to
see my mom now.

GIRL1: I tried to stop thinking of this picture I found but I
couldn't. It's a picture of my aunt holding me. I'm a baby and
we're at the hospital. But my mom said my aunt's been in
prison my whole life. I got a very bad feeling and— It can't
be my mom.

Sirens blare. Everyone reacts—

GIRL3: Something's happened!

GIRL2: Oh god . . . / There's an ambulance—

GIRL1: I have to know who my mom is—

GIRL3: My mom's / in trouble.

GIRL2: Someone's killed / themselves.

GIRL1: I have to know who / my mom is—

GIRL3: Something's happened to / my mom.

GIRL2: That's the only reason—

GIRL1: I have to know who my mom is—

GIRL2: I don't care about the / drugs—

GIRL1: I have to know who my mom is—

GIRL2: I don't care about / returning the jam.

GIRL3: I have a very bad / feeling—

GIRL1: I have to know who / my mom is—

GIRL2: Anything is better than dead.

GIRL3: I have to know if my mom is okay.

GIRL2: / I have to tell my mom—

GIRL1: / I have to know who my mom is.

GIRL3 looks at GIRL1.

GIRL3: What do you know?
GIRL1: Nothing.
GIRL3: Nothing?
GIRL1: I heard the words code yellow.
GIRL3: CODE YELLOW—that's hostage, HOSTAGE. When?
GIRL1: Earlier—I don't. Before. I've never been here before. I don't know.

GIRL1 starts to cry.

GIRL3: Stop crying!
GIRL1: Please don't yell at me!

GIRL2: The door opens. A guard walks in. She looks at me. She's shaking. She tells me I have to leave. NO! I have to see my mom!

GIRL1 / GIRL3: The door opens and a police officer appears.

GIRL2: I HAVE TO TELL HER!

GIRL3: He doesn't say anything.
GIRL1: He looks at me.

GIRL2: I have to tell my mom. Please! I have to tell her my truth! That it stops here. I have to tell her that it's going to stop here!

GIRL2 touches her belly.

GIRL1 / GIRL2 / GIRL3: NO MORE WAITING!

Lights out on GIRL2 and GIRL3. GIRL1 is alone in the light.

GIRL1: . . . Me?

GIRL1 gets up and heads towards the shadow of the door.

The officer says, "This way." I feel like I can't breathe. Like running in the winter.

He says, "I need you to be brave." I feel like a dead Christmas tree. Like, if you shook me, all my needles would fall out. He takes me outside and then inside again. Through the metal detectors again, and they pat me down again, and then inside through these cells, it's awful, people are going crazy, they're hitting things and crying and there's police wearing armour and I feel like I am floating. The guard takes my arm 'cause my legs have gone numb. I keep wishing that my dad would walk in and pick me up. Pick me up. Pick me up. Pick me up. Then I see.

GIRL1 freezes.

Lights up on KIT. She's holding a knife against the GUARD's throat.

GUARD: LOOK.

KIT sees GIRL1. GIRL1 sees KIT. KIT reaches her other arm out towards GIRL1, who is SID, her daughter.

KIT: My baby . . . Sidney.

GIRL1 / SID starts to slowly raise her hand and reach out as well. Then the wall of buckets shake.

SID turns and looks out at the audience.

SID: Well, I guess I would say it all started when I found out my mother wasn't my mother.

All the buckets tip over, spilling sports bras, pencils, tampons, knives, green beans, stuffed Minnie Mouses, baby soothers, calculators, chocolate wrappers, notebooks, drugs, tea bags, Pepsi cans, cigarettes, and a Christmas wreath, flooding the floor.

FOUR

Lights shift to the GUARD. KIT, SID, *and* GIRL3
watch her.

GUARD: Once upon a time there was a woman.

The GUARD *looks at the mess of the stage and then
goes to clean up.*

This woman had a daughter. It was just the two of them.
They lived in a queendom of their own creation. They liked
to sit under a big blanket and watch mystery shows on the
TV together. They lived in a city surrounded by a fortress of
traffic. The woman worked at a prison. A prison that took
women from all over the vast land.

One day, when the woman's daughter was thirteen, there
was an incident.

The GUARD *shifts her body and voice to be* KIT.

"It repeats. That's the one and only important thing that I've
learned here. It all repeats again."

An inmate held the woman hostage for seven hours.

She aggressively cleans.

If their life had been a TV show the woman would have come out of that experience shaken but determined to seize the rest of her days. She would have grabbed her daughter and said, "This, this is what's important." But life is not TV.

After the incident nothing was the same. Their life together split into happily befores and everything afters. The woman sat on their couch and smoked. The daughter tried to help her. She read all the spells and tried all the potions on PTSD but the woman hid in a giant tower of moods that her daughter was not allowed into.

The GUARD *gets caught staring at an object. A soother. She stops.*

Then, nine months later, the woman announced that she was going back to work. Her daughter begged her not to go back. To that prison. But the woman said that being afraid was letting them win. And she could never let them win again. The daughter never understood that.

She shifts to be GIRL3 */ her daughter.*

"You can't win or lose just by feeling something."

She picks up a tea bag, a green bean, a cigarette, a Pepsi can, and throws them into a bucket. Each object now affecting her.

So the woman went back to work and the daughter became a sorceress, removing the smell of cigarettes out of furniture. The daughter no longer made tea for her mother and they stopped watching TV together. Eventually, six years after the incident, the daughter journeyed away from her mother, leaving the woman alone.

She picks up a long, thin piece of fabric and puts it in a bucket.

That same year a nineteen-year-old girl was transferred to the prison that the women still worked at. There was something about this girl. She had no wishes left, she ate all the apples, she wouldn't wake, she acted out—

She shifts to be SID.

"There's a picture. I was tall . . . Do you remember me?"

The girl killed herself while the woman watched. No. Froze. The woman had wanted to move. She had wanted to save the girl. She had tried to save her, but she got stuck watching. Watching herself and the girl from a distance. And then it was too late.

When the police came, the woman was asked to wait, in a little room. But in the room there was another girl. Screaming about her mother. And for a moment she couldn't tell the difference between any girl she'd ever seen and any story she'd ever heard—

She shifts to be GIRL2.

"I have to tell her! It stops here. Please. I have to tell her *(touches her belly)* it's going to stop here!"

The GUARD can no longer clean up. She stops and stands perfectly still.

The woman ran. Out of the room. Into the parking lot. Into her car. She sped home. At home. She wanted tea—she put the kettle on—she thought she was okay—she's okay—but as the kettle screamed she heard—

"You be me."

And as the water boiled to nothing—

She looks at KIT.

She tried.

She looks at SID.

I tried.

She looks at GIRL3.

I'm trying.

She squeezes her eyes shut. Trying to be all of them. GIRL3 moves towards the GUARD till she is standing next to her. Then KIT does the same. Then SID. The four women stand together as the GUARD opens her eyes—

I remember.

Then the leak, from the ceiling, starts again, but this time grows. Water pours down on all four women and fills the stage.

Blackout.

ACKNOWLEDGEMENTS

I want to thank those who bravely and graciously spoke to me about their experience with Correctional Service Canada. A special thank you to Matt White, who asked me to explore this world with him and who nourished this play from its creation. Thank you to the journalists who have written about and continue to question the use of solitary confinement in this country; the Elizabeth Fry society and Senator Kim Pate for their outstanding work and support of this play; Richard Rose for his incredible attention to detail; and Audrey Dwyer, Derrick Chua, Pam Winters, Natasha Greenblatt, Esther Jun, Jo-Anne Corbeil, Stuart Grant, Joanna Falck, Andrea Romaldi, Tamara Podemski, Nick Storring, André du Toit, Joanna Yu, Nina Lee Aquino, Carin Lowerison, and Natasha Bean-Smith for their valuable insights. A huge thank you to Colin Rivers for navigating it all with me. Thank you to Green Light Arts for your incredible outreach in the community and to Tarragon Theatre for supporting me so completely in this play's premiere.

Thank you to my father for the way you listen to me and respond to my work. Thank you to my husband for bringing me back to my original love of theatre, for being down to talk it all out, and for sneakily making me very happy.

Thank you to my mother, who I ache for, and to that ache, which anchors everything I write. Thank you to my son, Dash, for coming into this world screaming hope.

Finally, I want to thank the original cast of this play. Vivien Endicott-Douglas—writing this role for you was the greatest gift; you are my best friend and great muse. Virgilia Griffith—my pisces girl—I met you on day one when I had nothing but an idea; your sensitivity, intellect, and sheer talent grew this play with me. Michaela Washburn—my words and heart have always been searching for you; I was able to finish this play because of you. Columpa C. Bobb—I will always be grateful that your patience, integrity, and brilliance found this play when it did. Thank you. You are all my creative bests.

Charlotte Corbeil-Coleman is a Governor General's Literary Award–nominated playwright and winner of the Dora Mavor Moore Award, the Herman Voaden National Playwriting Competition, and the K.M. Hunter Artist Award. She graduated from the playwriting program at the National Theatre School and writes for theatre, radio, film, and television. Her writing includes *The End of Pretending* with Emily Sugerman, *Twisted* with Joseph Jomo Pierre, *Scratch*, and *Sudden Death*. She directed and co-created *Highway 63: The Fort Mac Show* and wrote for CBC Radio's *Afghanada* and for the TV series *King*. Currently she is developing two new musicals. She lives in Toronto.

First edition: October 2019
Printed and bound in Canada by Rapido Books, Montreal

Jacket art, *Big Lots* [oil and acrylic on wooden panel,
51 x 40.5 cm, 2012], © 2012 by Amanda Rhodenizer,
www.arhodenizer.com.
Author photo © Anne Bayin

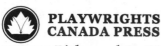 **PLAYWRIGHTS
CANADA PRESS**
202-269 Richmond St. W.
Toronto, ON
M5V 1X1

416.703.0013
info@playwrightscanada.com
www.playwrightscanada.com
@playcanpress